PIANO CHORDS
MADE EASY
by William Bay
MB22104
LARGE PRINT
EDITION

BILL'S MUSIC SHELF

2 **Table of Contents**

Table of Contents

How to Read Diagrams

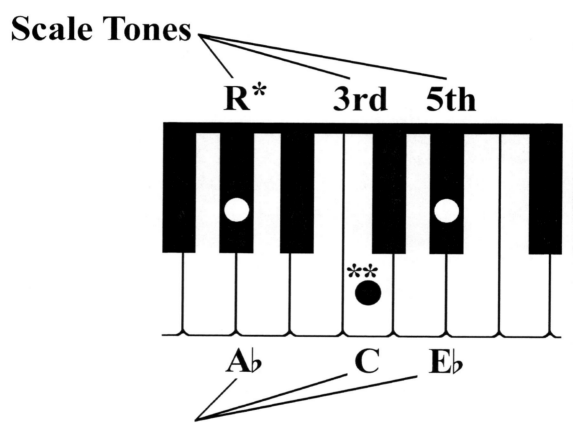

Scale Tones

R*   3rd   5th

A♭   C   E♭

Names of Notes in Chord

* R = Root or tonic note of chord.
** ○, ● = Keys to Play.

Major

C

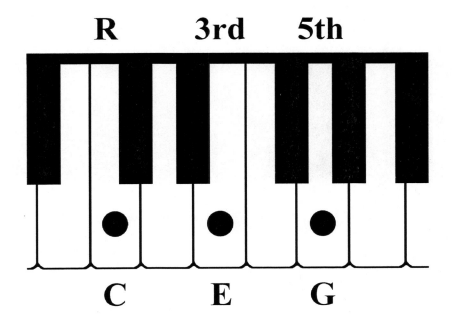

Major

F

R   3rd   5th

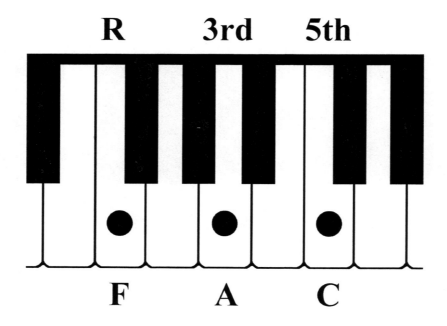

F   A   C

Major

B♭

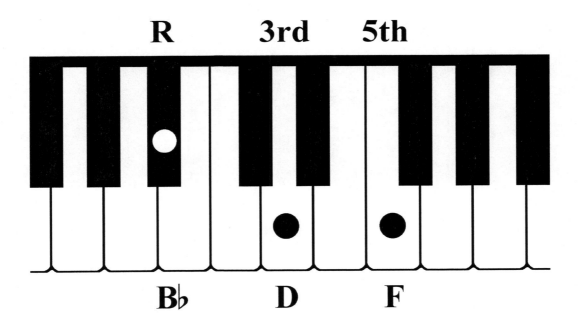

R   3rd   5th

B♭   D   F

Major

Eb

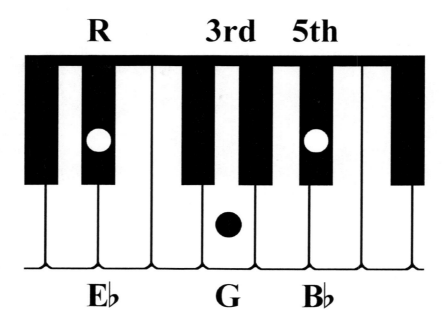

Major

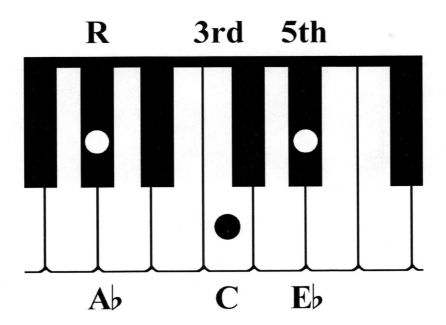

Major

Db

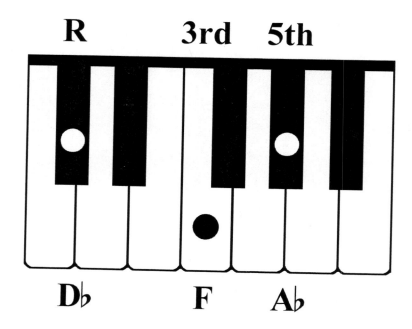

R   3rd   5th

Db   F   Ab

Major

F♯ / G♭

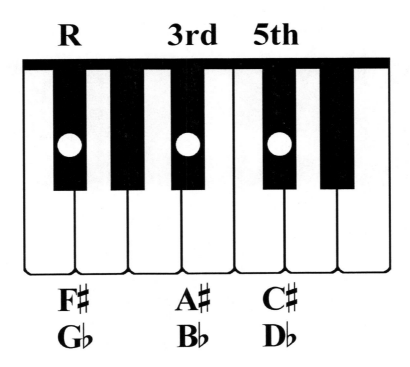

R   3rd   5th

F♯   A♯   C♯
G♭   B♭   D♭

Major

B

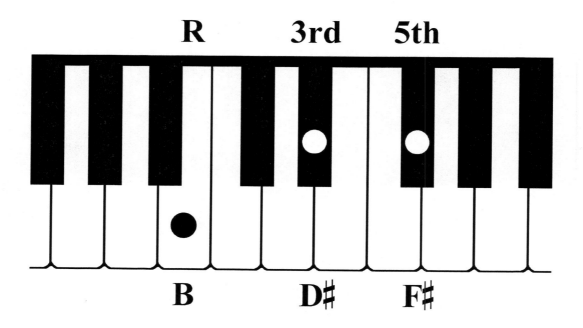

Major

E

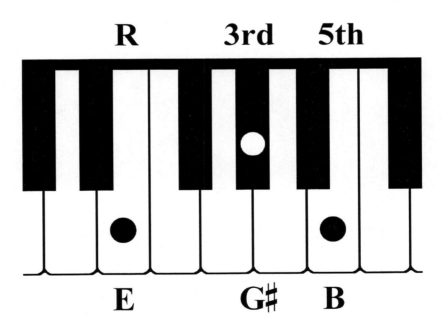

R   3rd   5th

E   G♯   B

Major

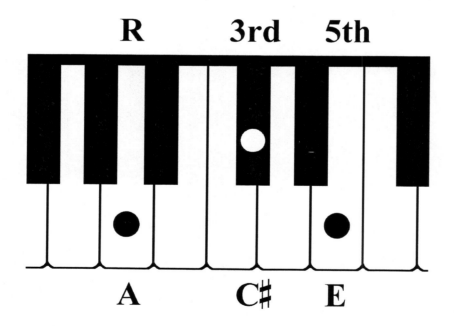

Major

D

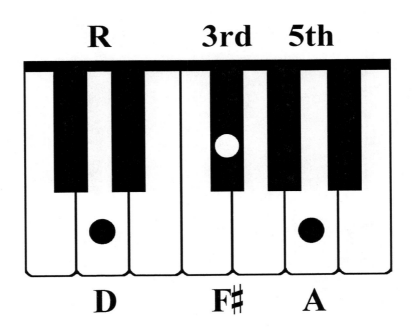

R   3rd   5th

D   F♯   A

Major

G

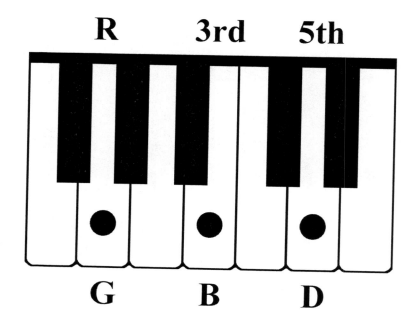

Minor

Cm

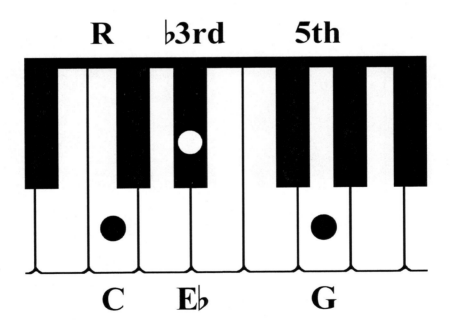

Minor

Fm

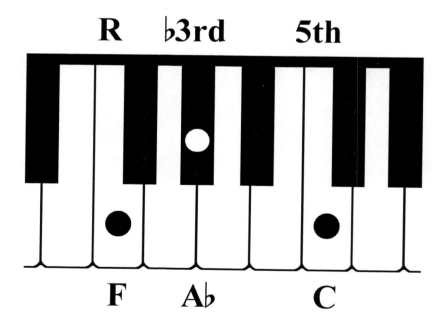

R   ♭3rd   5th

F   A♭   C

Minor

B♭m

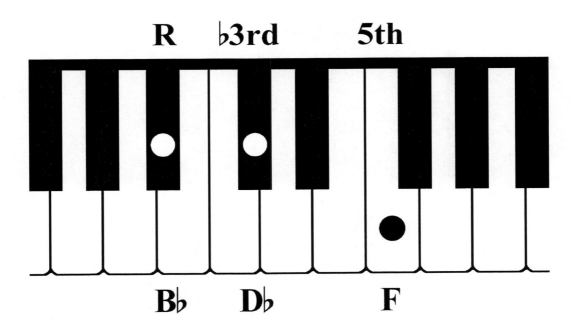

Minor

E♭m

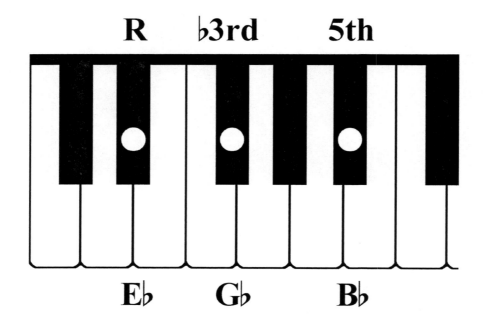

R   ♭3rd   5th

E♭   G♭   B♭

Minor

$A\flat m$

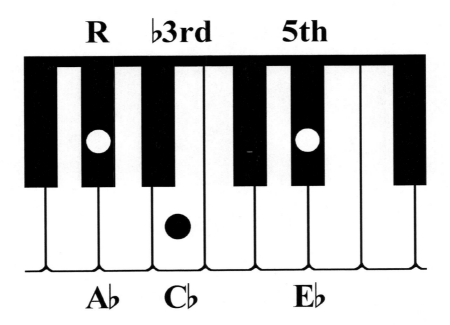

Minor

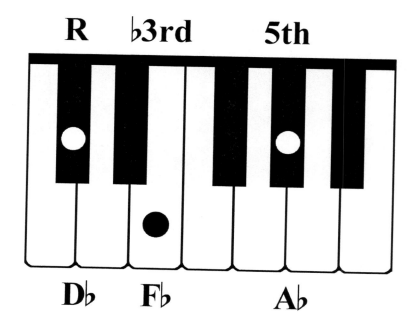

Minor

F#m / Gbm

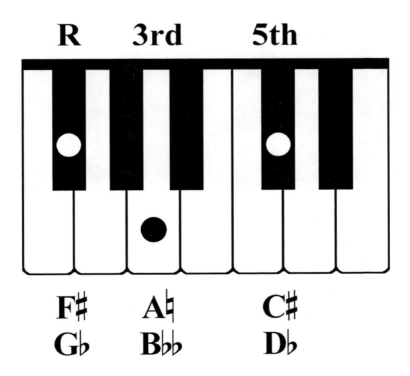

Minor

Bm

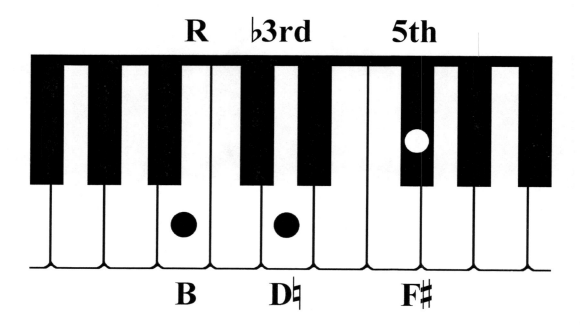

Minor

Em

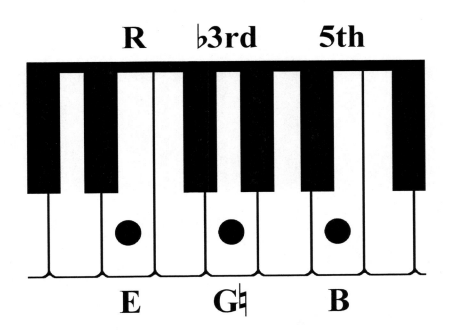

Minor

Am

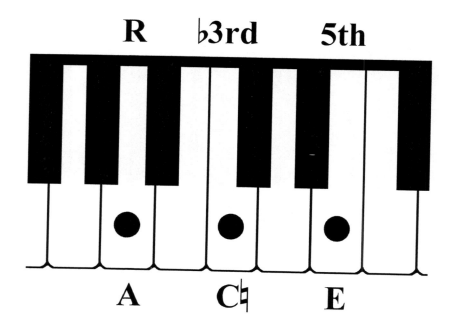

Minor

Dm

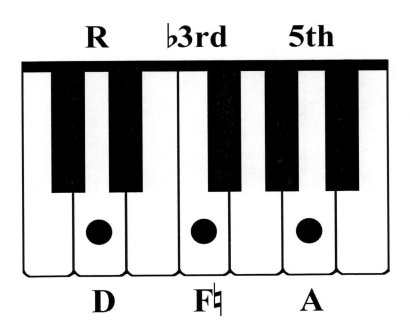

Minor

Gm

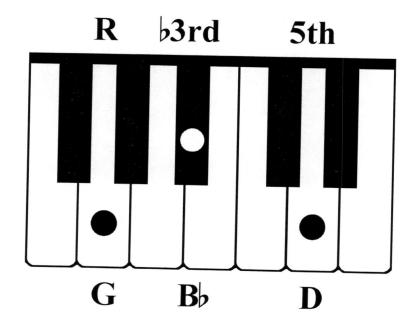

Seventh

C7

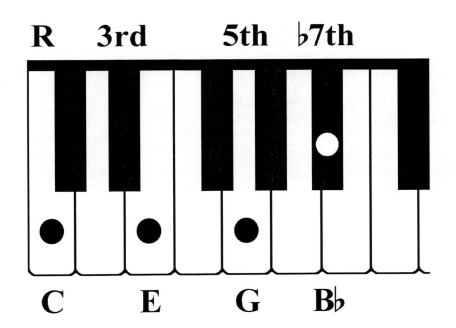

R   3rd   5th   ♭7th

C   E   G   B♭

Seventh

F7

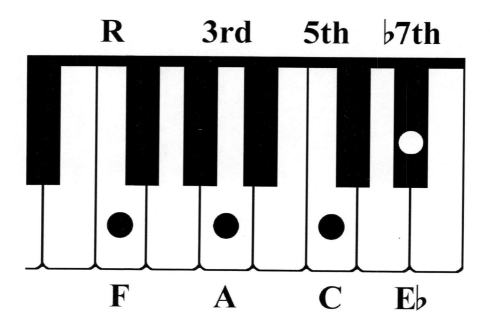

R   3rd   5th   ♭7th

F   A   C   E♭

Seventh

B♭7

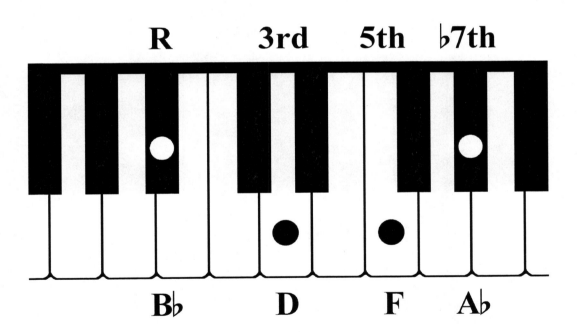

R   3rd   5th   ♭7th

B♭   D   F   A♭

Seventh

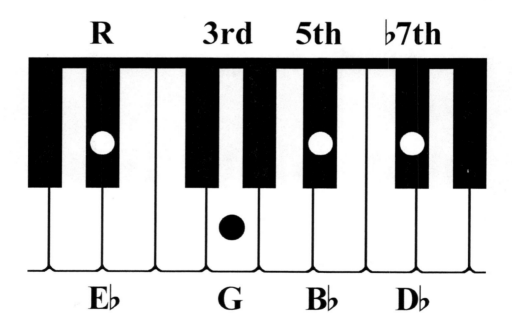

Seventh

$$A\flat 7$$

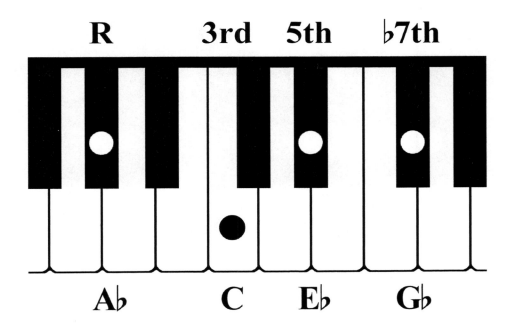

R   3rd   5th   ♭7th

A♭   C   E♭   G♭

Seventh

Db7

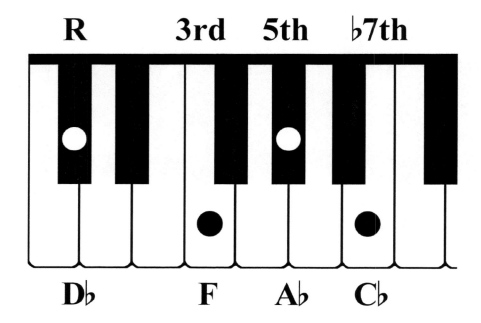

Seventh

$$\boxed{\textbf{F}\sharp\textbf{7}/\textbf{G}\flat\textbf{7}}$$

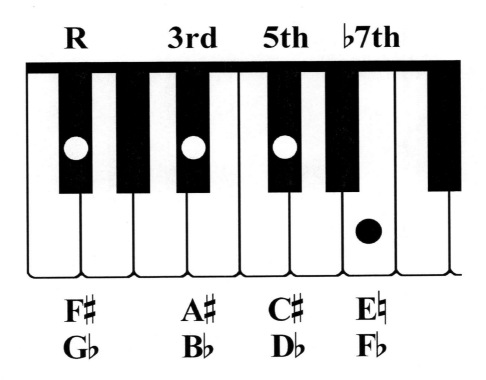

Seventh

B7

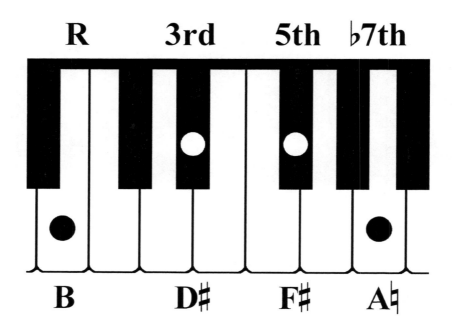

R   3rd   5th   ♭7th

B   D♯   F♯   A♮

Seventh

E7

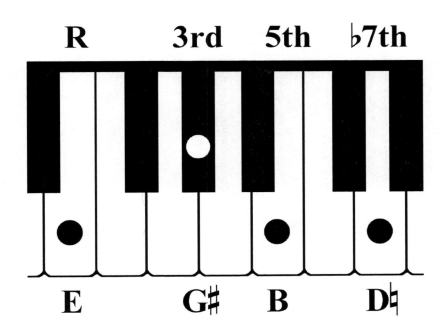

Seventh

A7

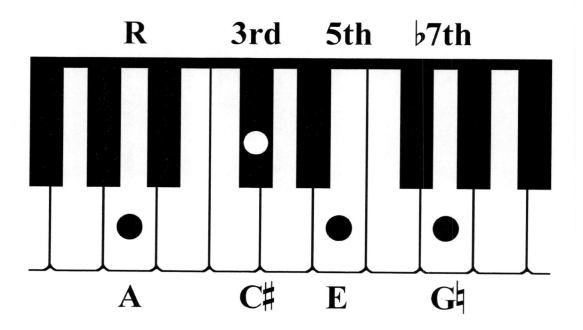

Seventh

D7

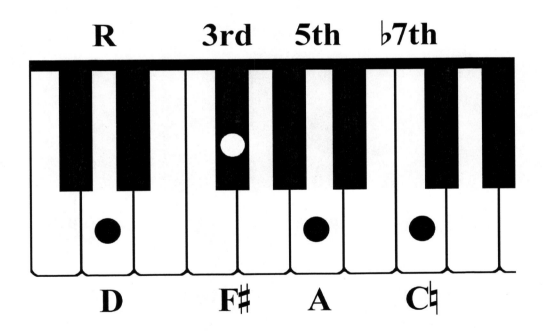

Seventh

G7

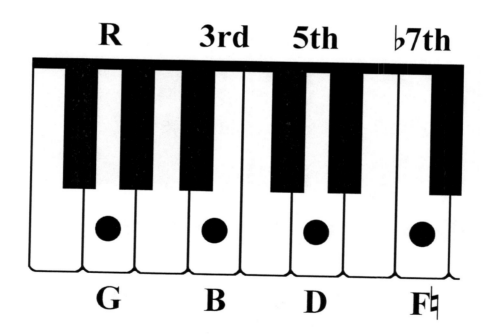

Minor 7th

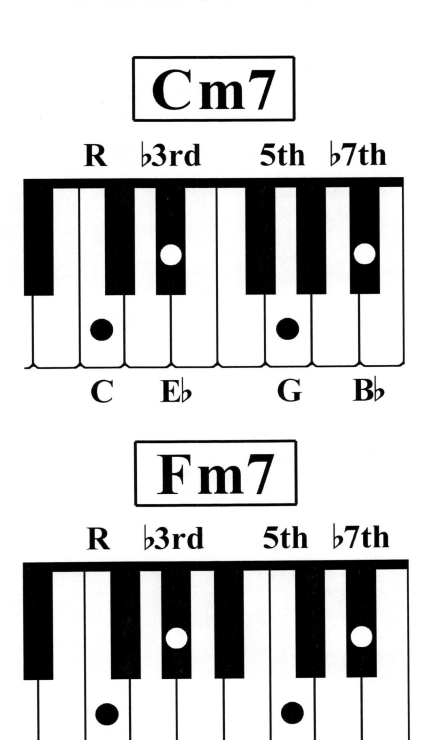

Minor 7th

Bbm7

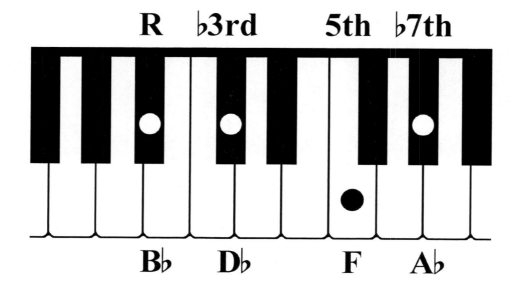

R   b3rd   5th   b7th

Bb   Db   F   Ab

Ebm7

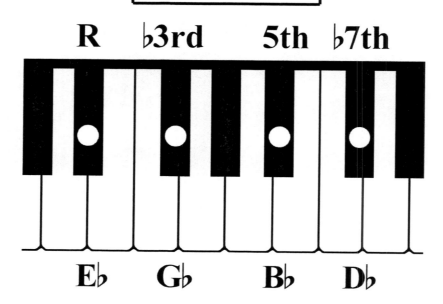

R   b3rd   5th   b7th

Eb   Gb   Bb   Db

Minor 7th

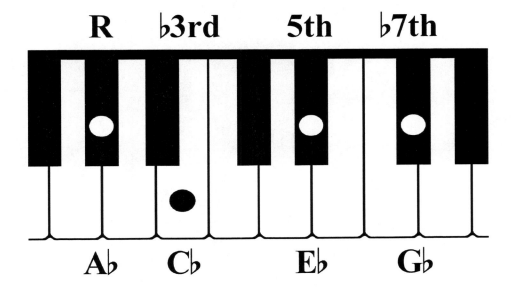

R	♭3rd	5th	♭7th
A♭	C♭	E♭	G♭

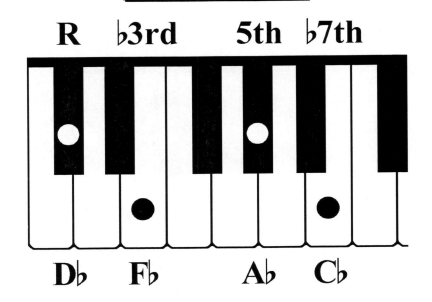

R	♭3rd	5th	♭7th
D♭	F♭	A♭	C♭

Minor 7th

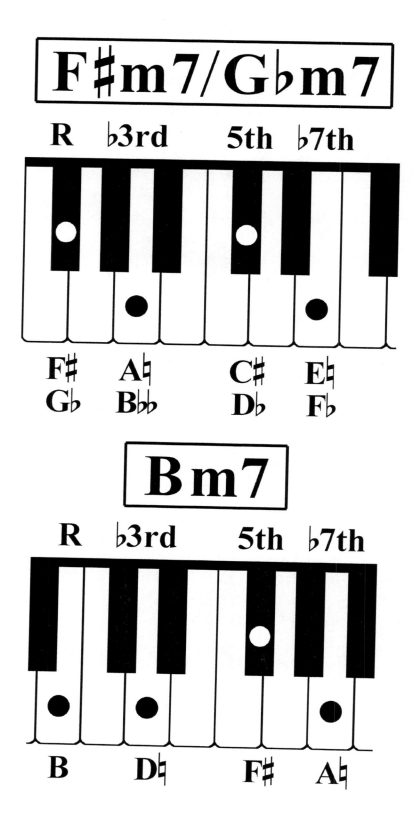

Minor 7th

Em7

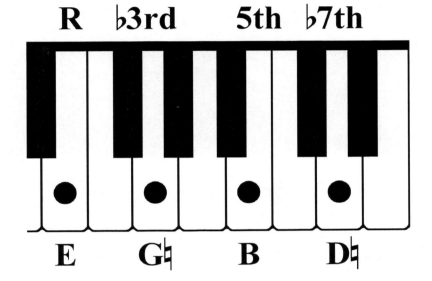

R   ♭3rd   5th   ♭7th

E   G♮   B   D♮

Am7

R   ♭3rd   5th   ♭7th

A   C♮   E   G♮

Minor 7th

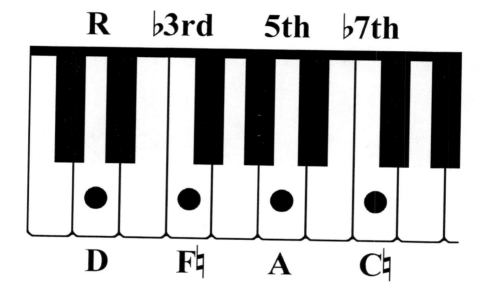

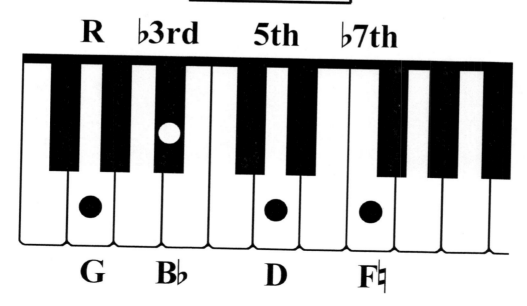

Major 7th

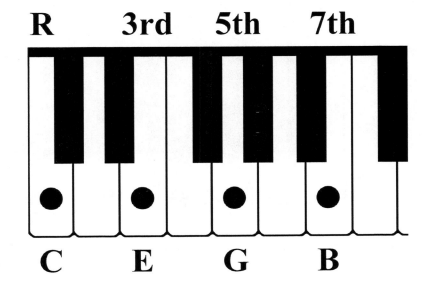

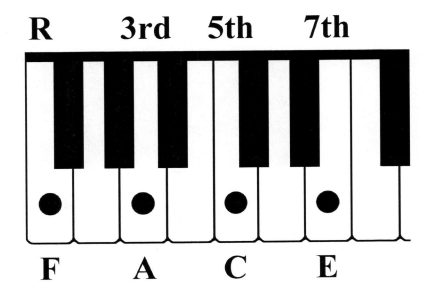

Major 7th

B♭ma7

R		3rd	5th		7th

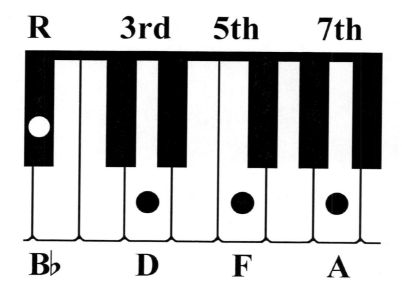

B♭   D   F   A

E♭ma7

R		3rd	5th		7th

E♭   G   B♭   D

Major 7th

A♭ma7

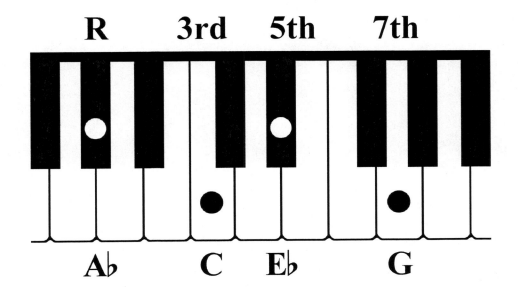

R   3rd   5th   7th

A♭   C   E♭   G

D♭ma7

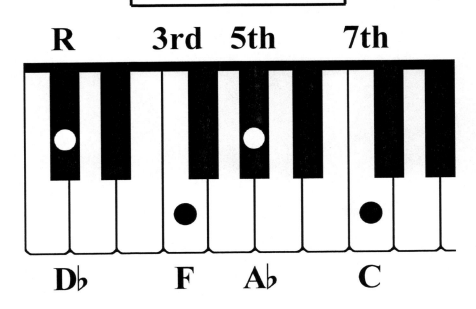

R   3rd   5th   7th

D♭   F   A♭   C

Major 7th

F#ma7/G♭ma7

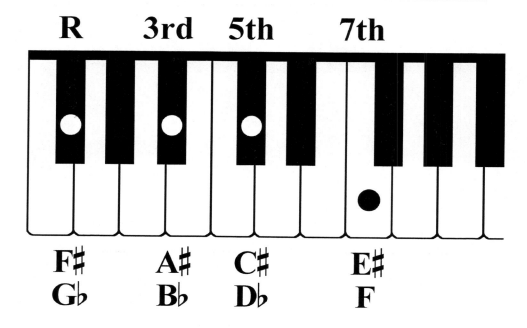

Bma7

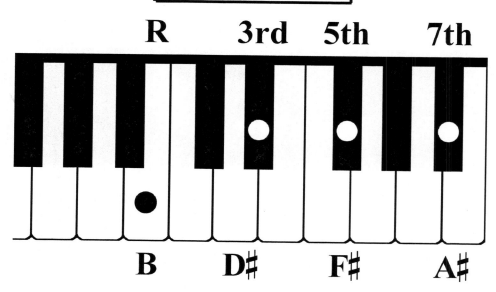

Major 7th

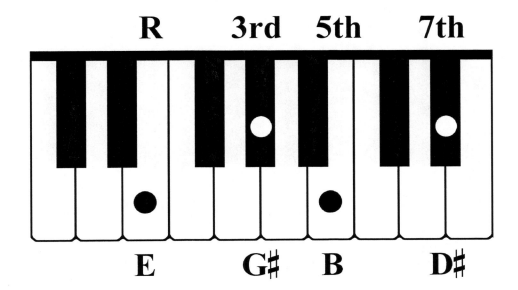

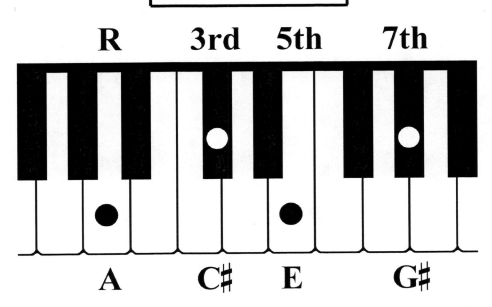

Major 7th

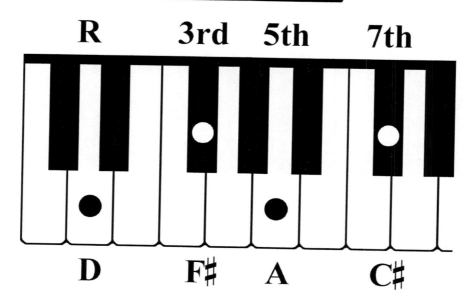

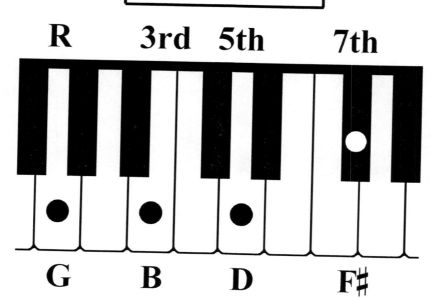

Sixth

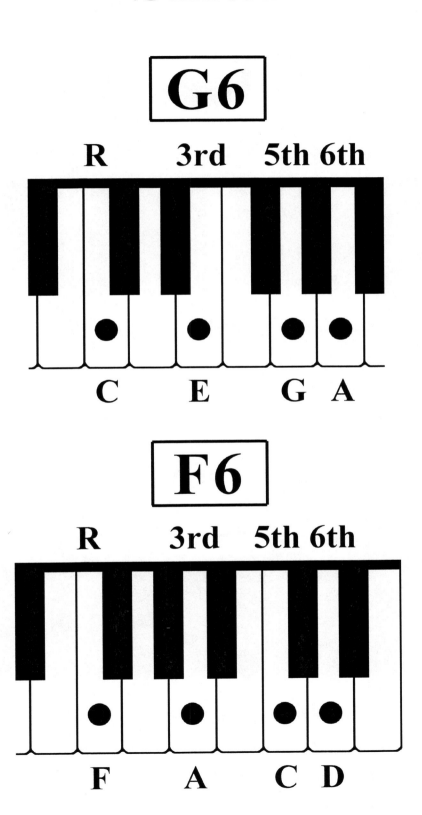

Sixth

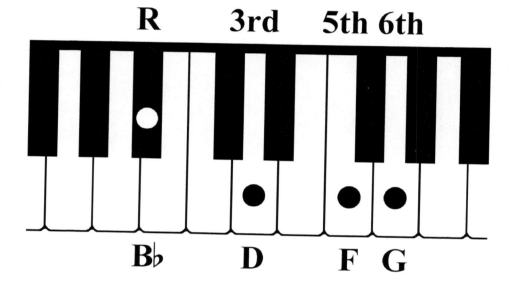

Sixth

R   3rd   5th 6th

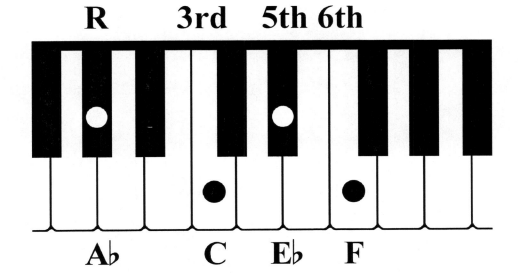

Ab   C   Eb   F

R   3rd   5th 6th

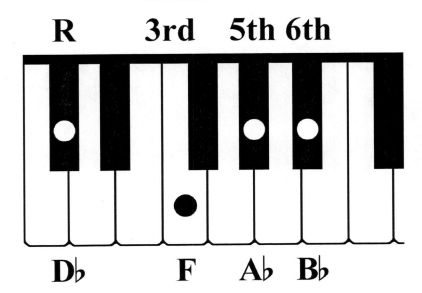

Db   F   Ab   Bb

Sixth

F#6 / G♭6

R	3rd	5th	6th

F#   A#   C#   D#
G♭   B♭   D♭   E♭

B6

R	3rd	5th	6th

B   D#   F#   G#

Sixth

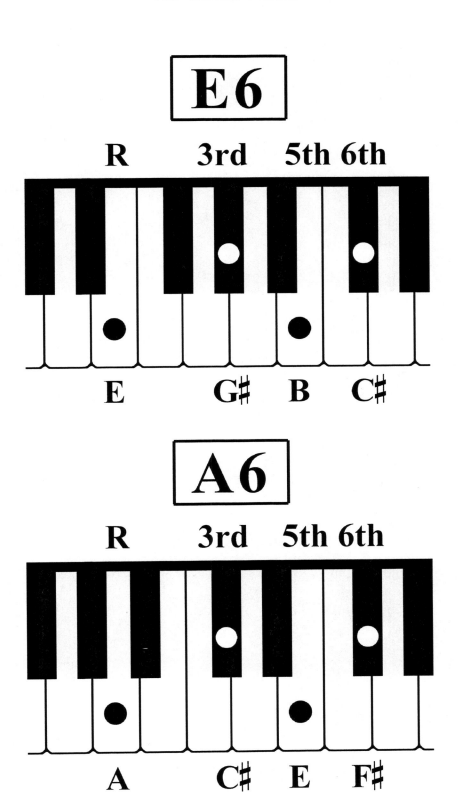

Sixth

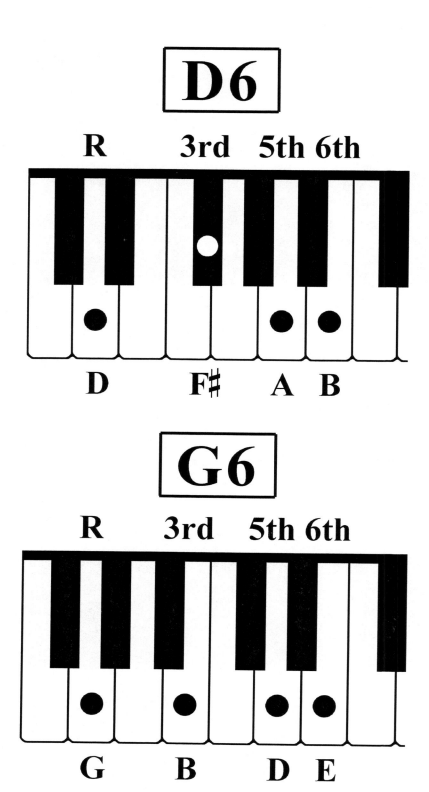

Minor 6th

R ♭3rd 5th 6th

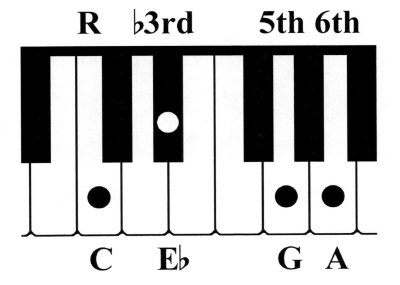

C E♭ G A

Fm6

R ♭3rd 5th 6th

F A♭ C D

Minor 6th

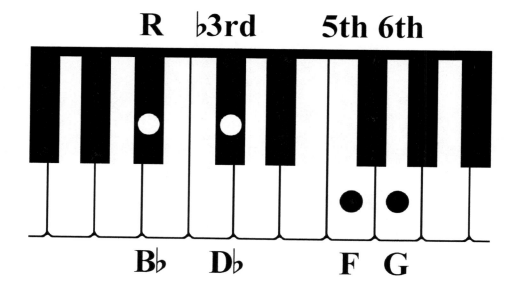

B♭m6

R   ♭3rd   5th 6th

B♭   D♭   F   G

E♭m6

R   ♭3rd   5th 6th

E♭   G♭   B♭ C

Minor 6th

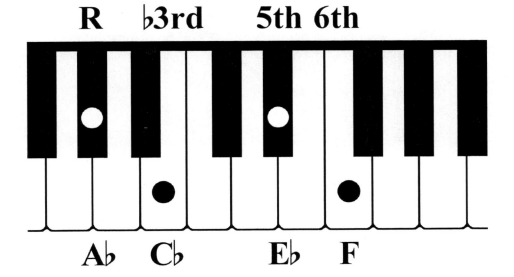

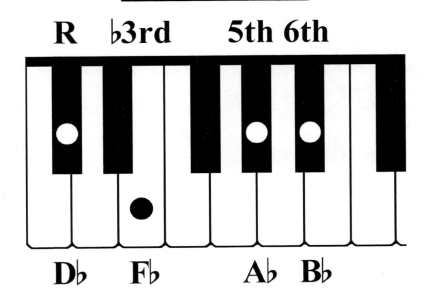

Minor 6th

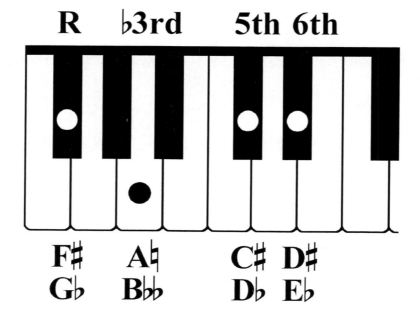

F♯m6 / G♭m6

R	♭3rd		5th	6th

F♯   A♮   C♯   D♯
G♭   B♭♭   D♭   E♭

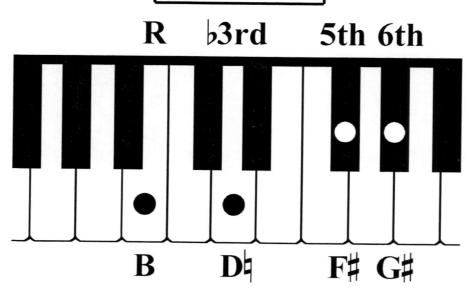

Bm6

R	♭3rd		5th	6th

B   D♮   F♯   G♯

Minor 6th

Em6

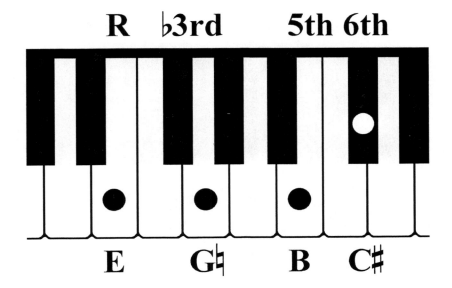

R   ♭3rd   5th   6th

E   G♮   B   C♯

Am6

R   ♭3rd   5th   6th

A   C♮   E   F♯

Minor 6th

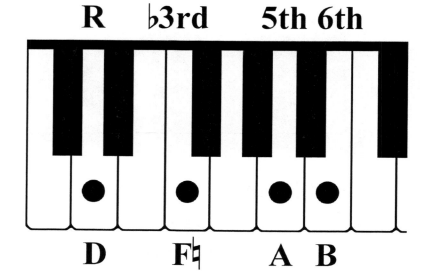

R ♭3rd 5th 6th

D F♮ A B

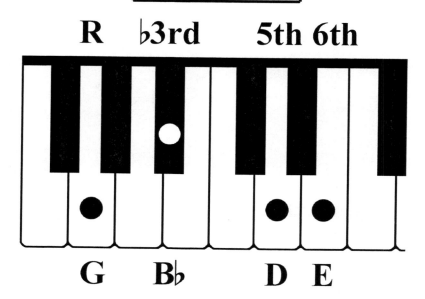

R ♭3rd 5th 6th

G B♭ D E

Diminished 7th

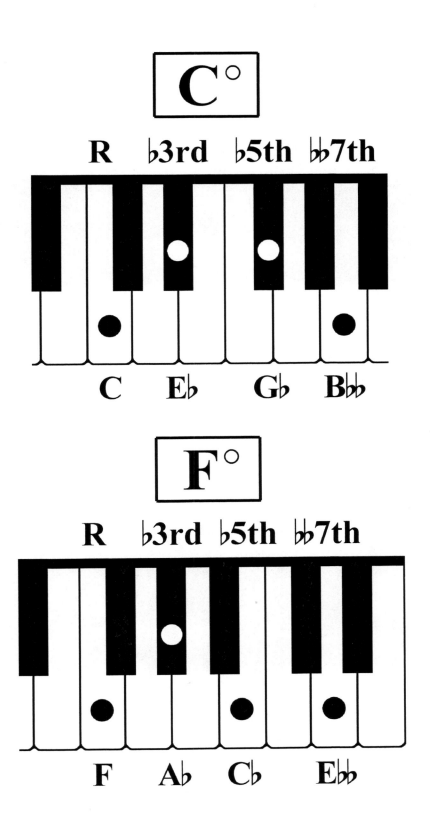

Diminished 7th

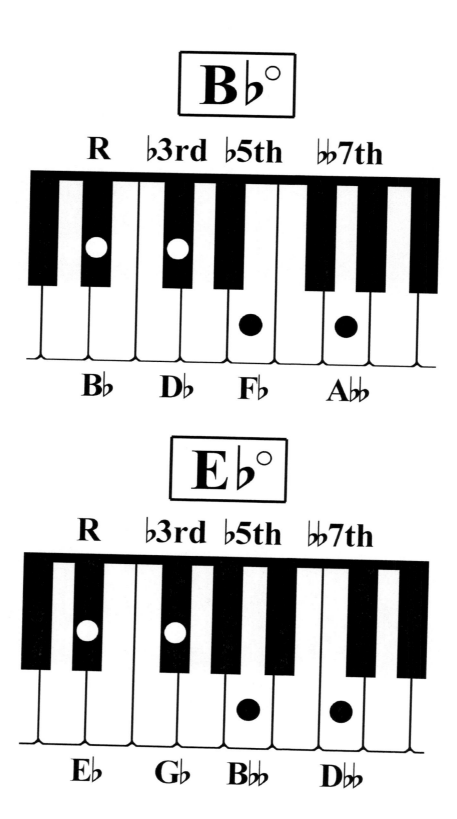

Diminished 7th

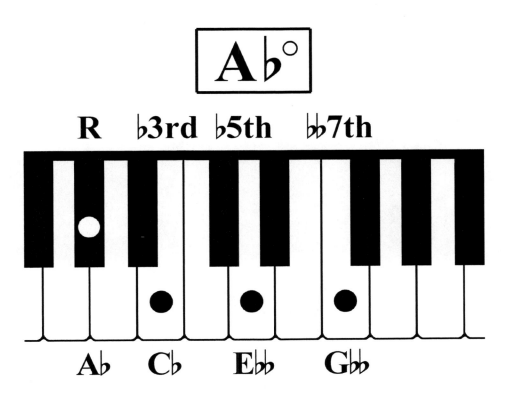

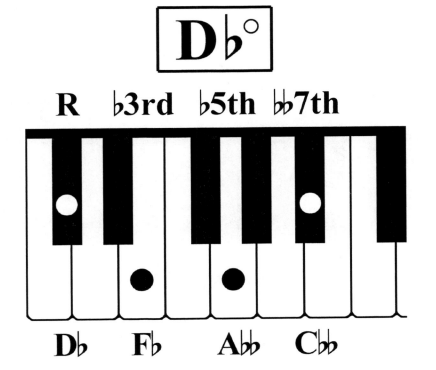

Diminished 7th

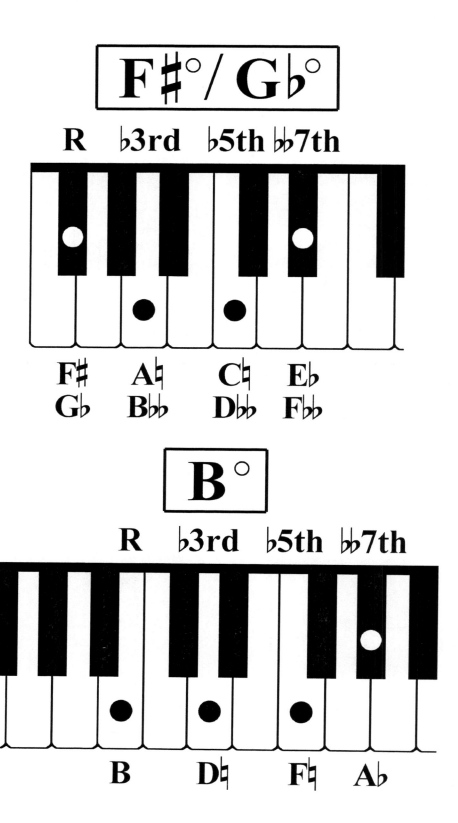

Diminished 7th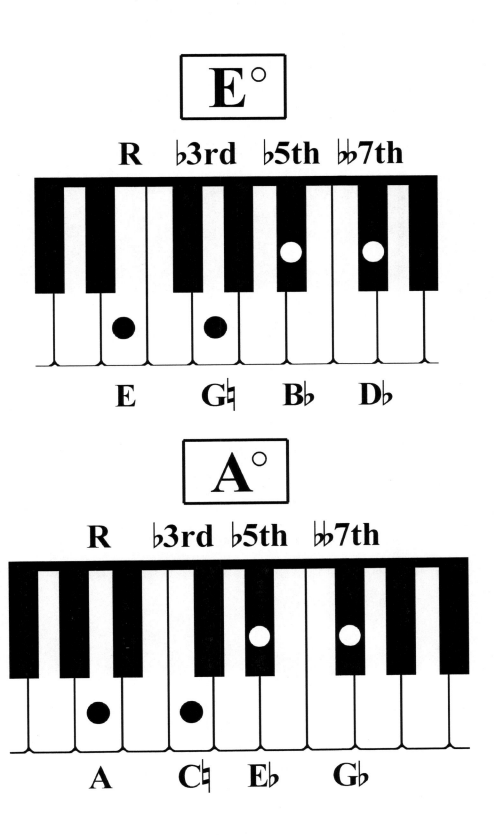

Diminished 7th

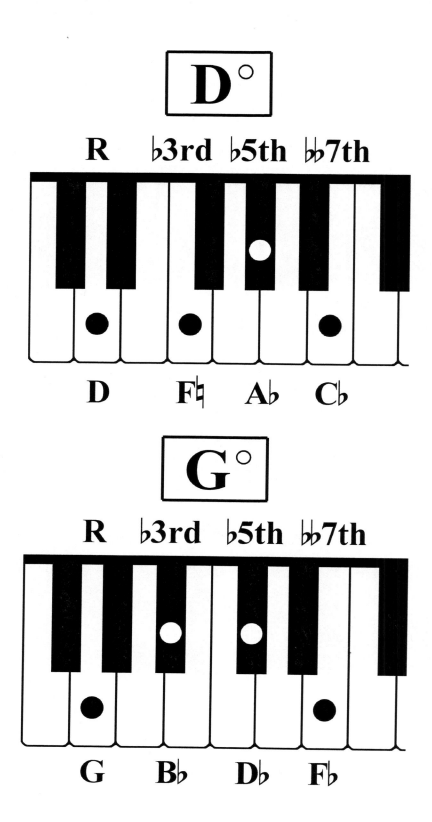

Augmented

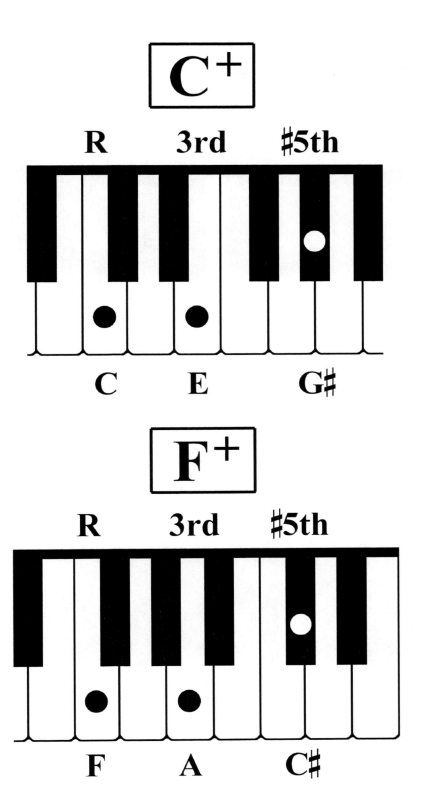

Augmented

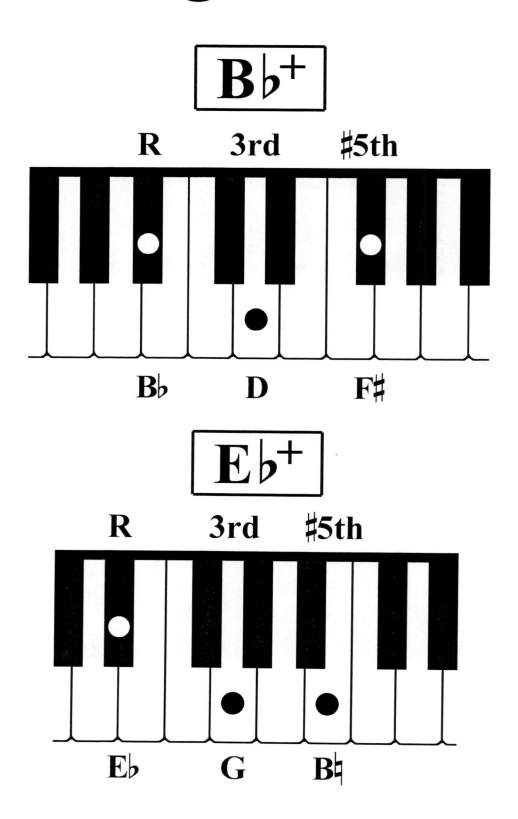

Augmented

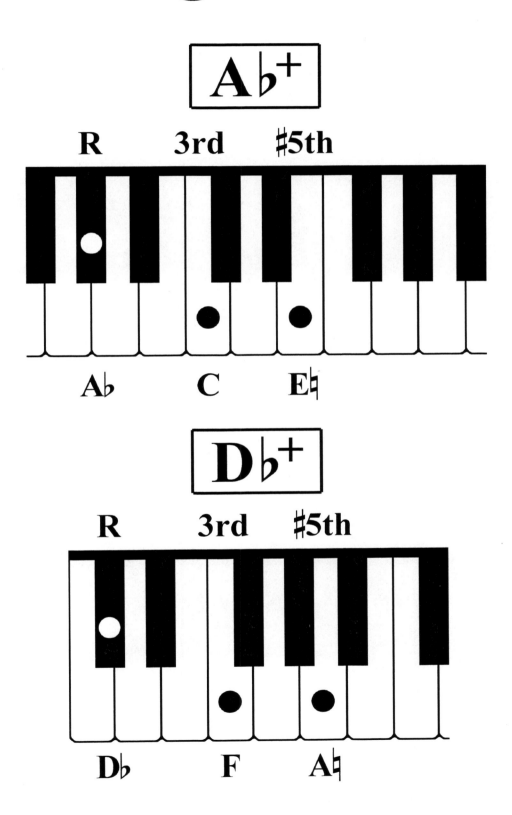

Augmented

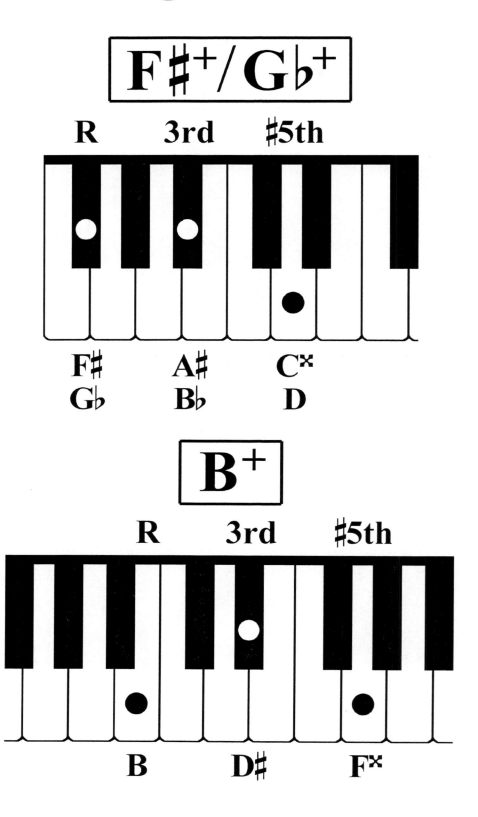

Augmented

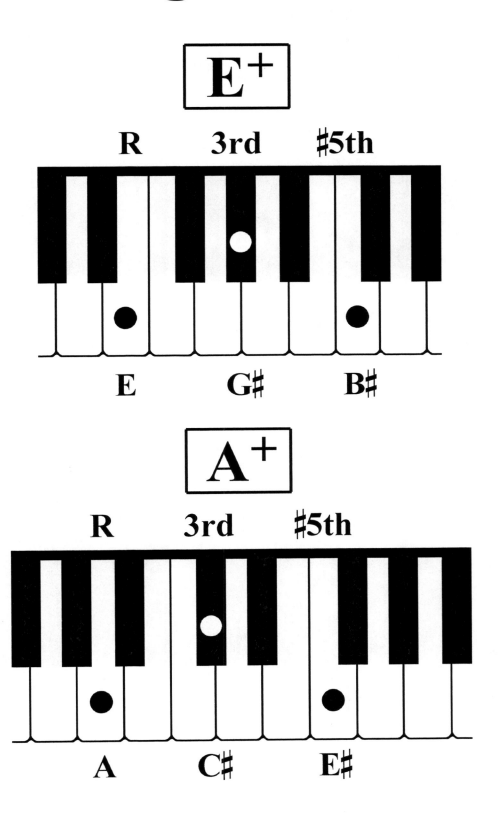

Augmented

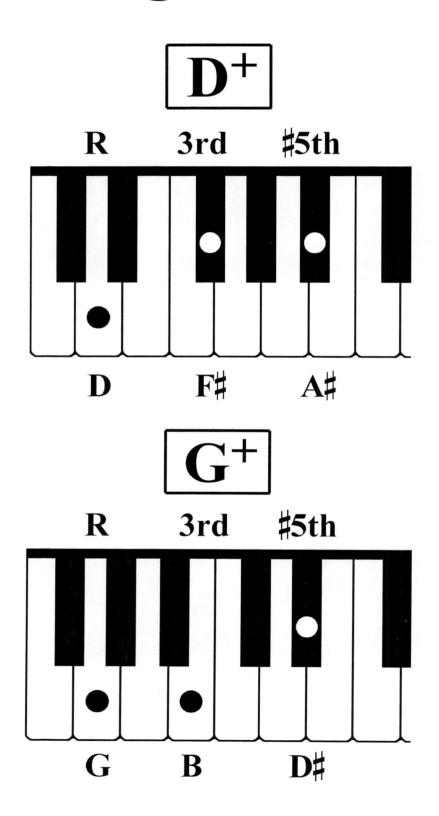

7♯5

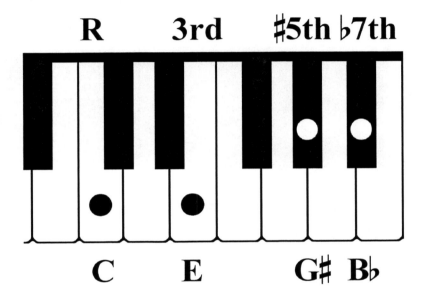

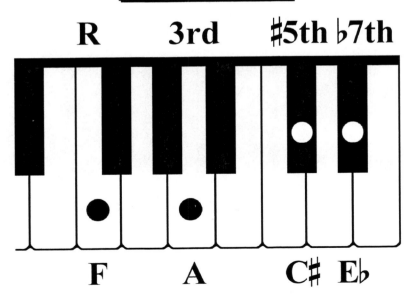

7♯5

B♭7♯5

R   3rd   ♯5th ♭7th

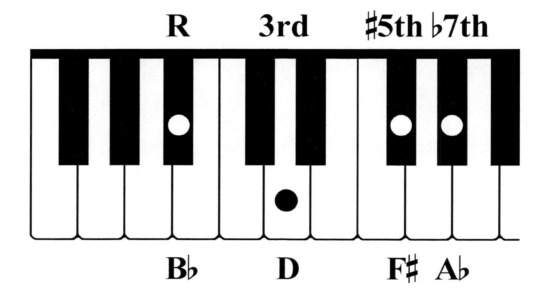

B♭   D   F♯ A♭

E♭7♯5

R   3rd   ♯5th ♭7th

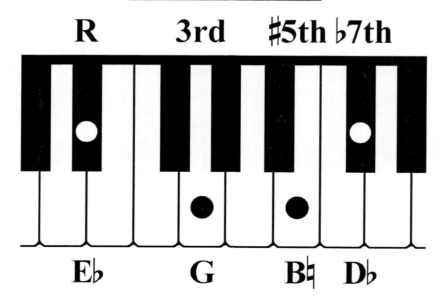

E♭   G   B♮ D♭

7♯5

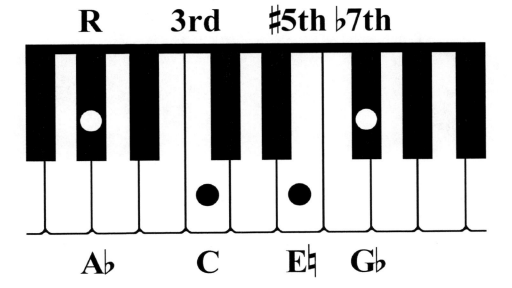

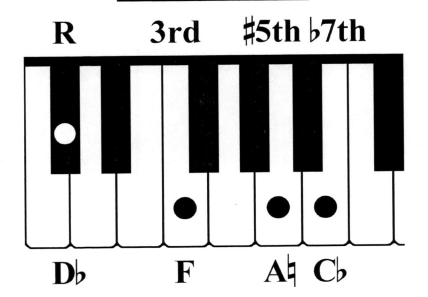

7♯5

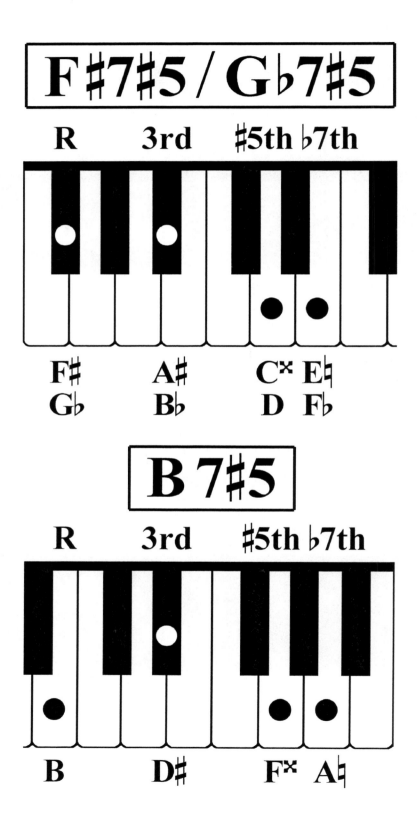

F♯7♯5 / G♭7♯5

R   3rd   ♯5th ♭7th

F♯   A♯   C𝄪 E♮
G♭   B♭   D F♭

B 7♯5

R   3rd   ♯5th ♭7th

B   D♯   F𝄪 A♮

7♯5

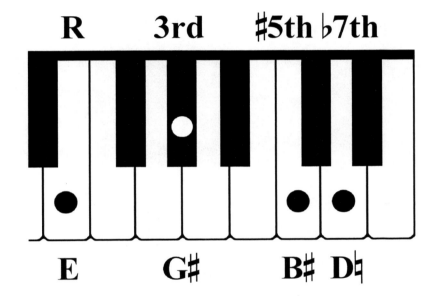

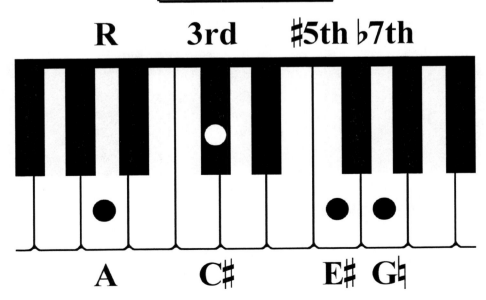

7♯5

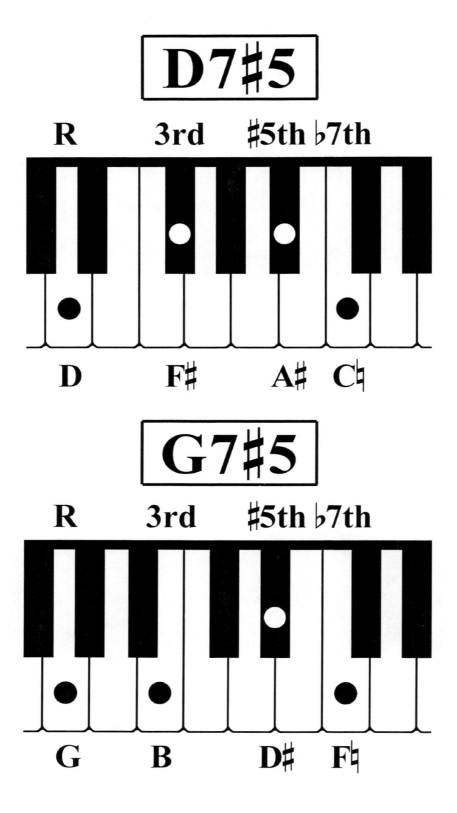

7♭5

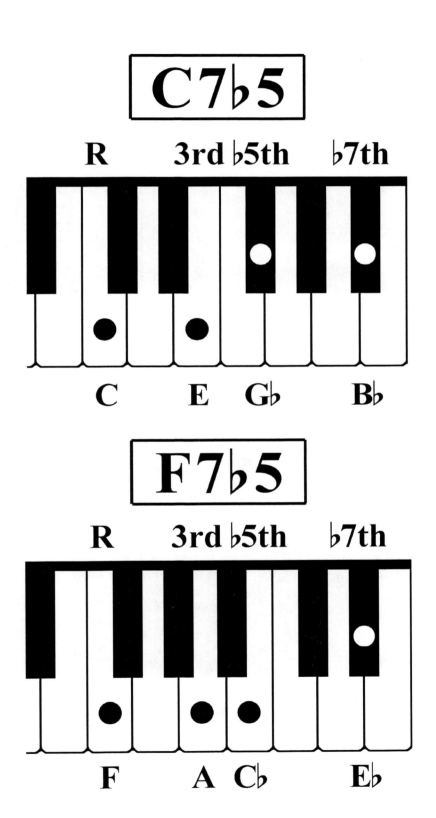

7♭5

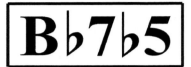

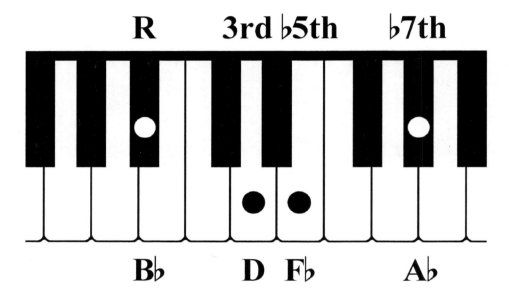

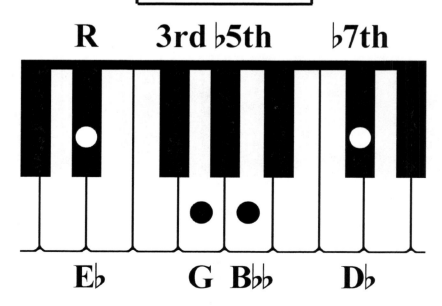

7♭5

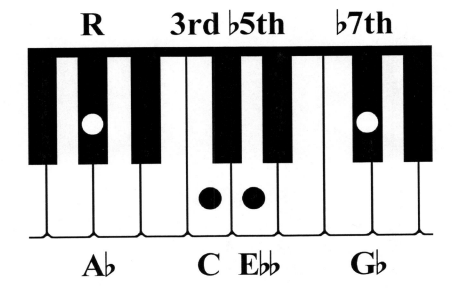

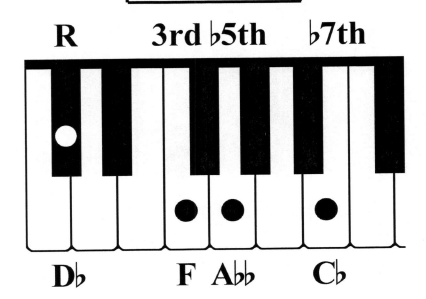

7♭5

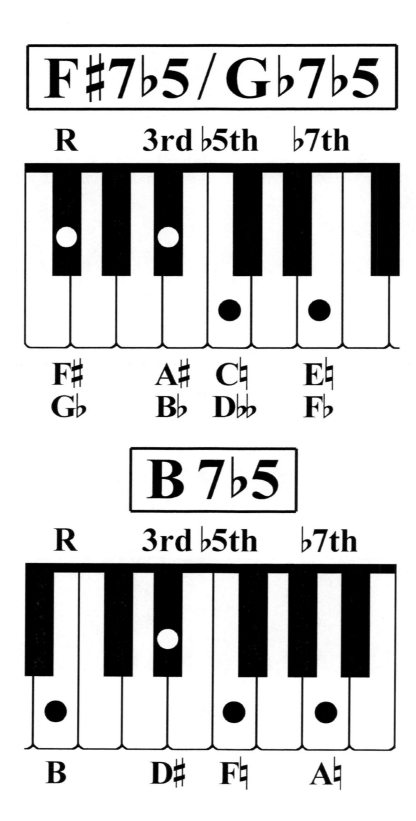

7♭5

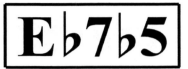

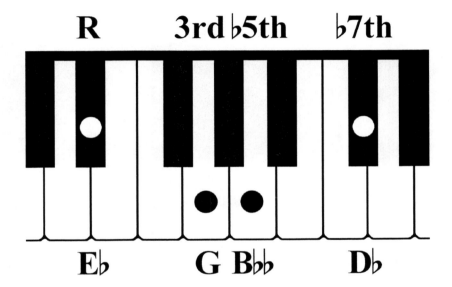

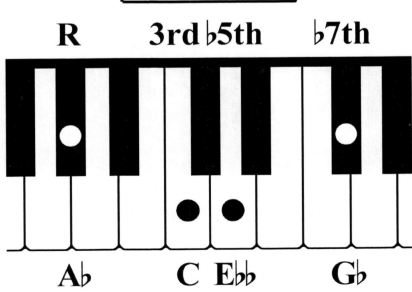

7♭5

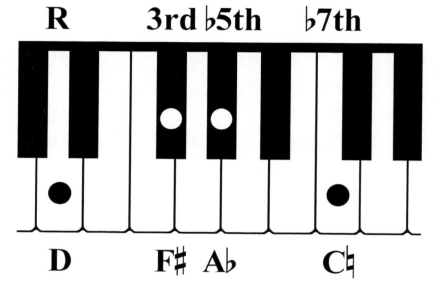

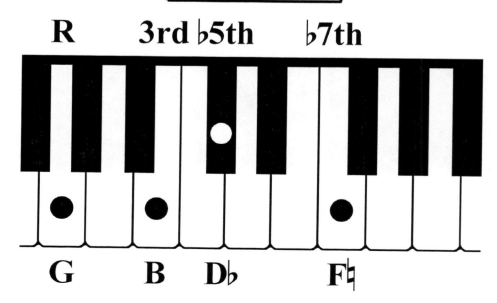

Minor7♭5

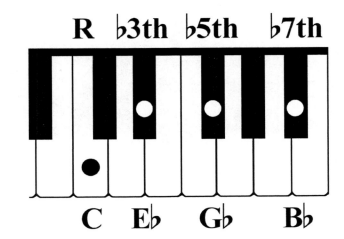

Cm7♭5

R   ♭3th   ♭5th   ♭7th

C   E♭   G♭   B♭

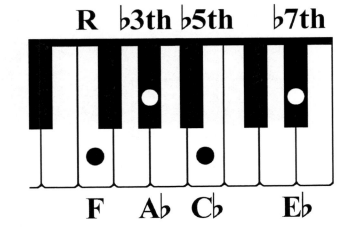

Fm7♭5

R   ♭3th ♭5th   ♭7th

F   A♭   C♭   E♭

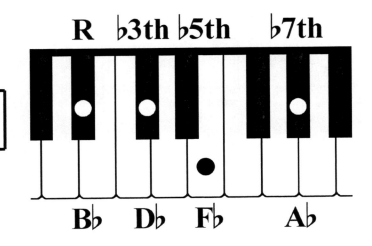

B♭m7♭5

R   ♭3th ♭5th   ♭7th

B♭   D♭   F♭   A♭

Minor7♭5

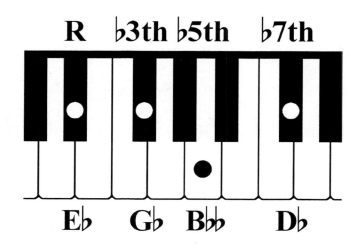

E♭m7♭5

R ♭3th ♭5th ♭7th

E♭ G♭ B♭♭ D♭

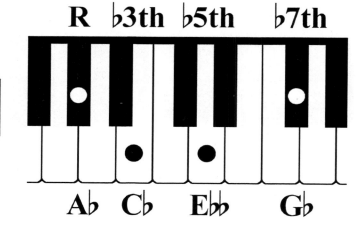

A♭m7♭5

R ♭3th ♭5th ♭7th

A♭ C♭ E♭♭ G♭

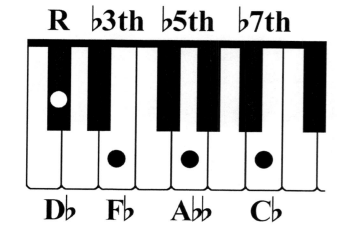

D♭m7♭5

R ♭3th ♭5th ♭7th

D♭ F♭ A♭♭ C♭

Minor7♭5

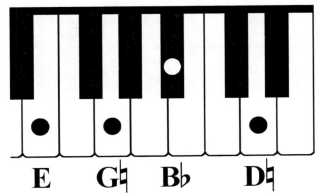

Minor7♭5

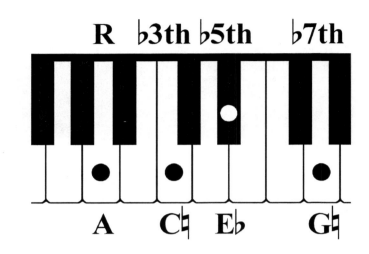

Am7♭5

R ♭3th ♭5th ♭7th

A C♮ E♭ G♮

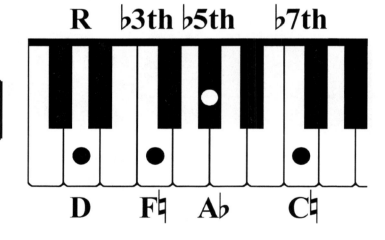

Dm7♭5

R ♭3th ♭5th ♭7th

D F♮ A♭ C♮

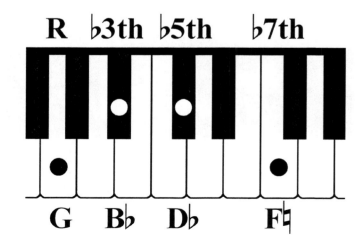

Gm7♭5

R ♭3th ♭5th ♭7th

G B♭ D♭ F♮

7th Suspended

C7sus

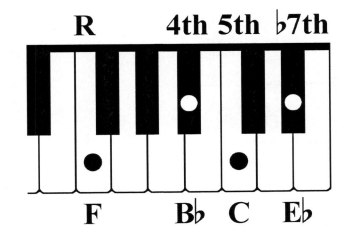

F7sus

Bb7sus

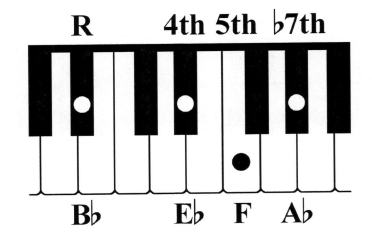

7th Suspended

E♭7sus

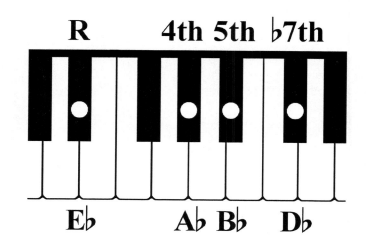

A♭7sus

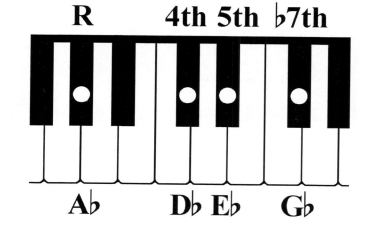

D♭7sus

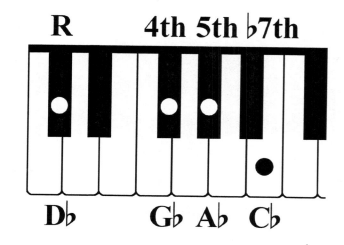

7th Suspended

F#7sus
Gb7sus

R   4th 5th b7th

F#   B C# E♮
Gb   Cb Db Fb

B 7sus

R   4th 5th b7th

B   E F# A♮

E 7sus

R   4th 5th b7th

E   A B D♮

7th Suspended

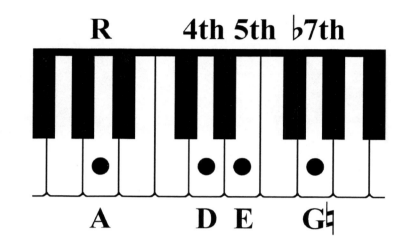

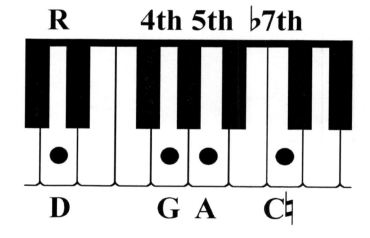

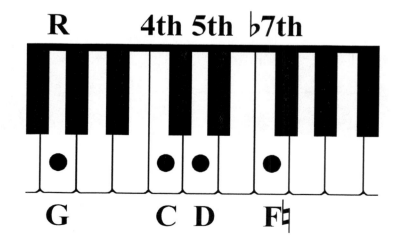